The Book of Thrones

The Book of Thrones

Marc Estafanous

Neurobaby Publishing
2019

Published 2019 by Neurobaby Publishing

First Printing: 2019

Graphic design and artwork by Jackie LoPresti

ISBN 978-1-7332619-0-6

Dedication

To my children, Lucas, Rachel and Mary, for whom I would do anything; especially if it results in embarrassing them.

Acknowledgments

I would like to thank my daughters, Rachel and Mary, for asking me to stop taking pictures over and over again, like they did with the beard styles, for accepting their fate as my children and jumping in to help when needed as photographers. Thanks to my father, brother and son, Fawzy, John and Lucas Estafanous, for tolerating my talking about the book, and supplying props and captions.

A very special, HUGE thank you to Jackie LoPresti who found, took, and contributed to so many of the pictures for her tenacity, time and availability. Thank her also for the editing, graphic design, artwork and the never ending creativity of hers that made this book so much better. I can't thank Jackie enough.

I want to sincerely thank Jessica French, who will always be a part of me, for being an amazing person, for always being up for shenanigans regardless of how tired she was, or how crazy she thought I was, as well as for taking the first pictures. A thank you also goes to Ken Bowman finding *Number 2* and suggesting the idea of the book. Thank you also Veronica Carkido for coming up with a great title, an Easter egg idea, and her find, pictures and props.

A special thank you goes to the original group: Jessica French, Ken Bowman, Chris Bowman, Dmitry Egorov, and Sonya Beardon. The group jump started this whole adventure.

Thank you of course to the rest of the photographers, finders, prop suppliers, and the people who came up with captions and titles for their time and creativity: Tierra Sump, Bill Buehl-Reichard, Shirley Zimmerman, Kevin Adelstein, Heather Vance, Sammi Steindler, Jahadge Floyd, Veronica Carkido, Jill Hardy, Josh Zimmerman, Brian Kraig, John Abdelsayed, Cory Nichols, Dara Briggs, Nicol Mackall, Nicole Lortz, Troy Budgen, Stacy Nichols, Richard Marshall, Michael Dugan, Jen Trick, Phil Mansour, Melissa Howard, Donna Whitaker, Amanda Nagy, Kim Smith, Don Brinberg, Taryn Jeffers, Beth Nielsen,

Howard Krantz, and Andrew Smith. Special thanks go to Amanda Poole and Ashley Zieminick for their prolificness.

Finally, I'd like to thank those not mentioned above who enjoyed the pictures or joined the caption and title contest for making the whole thing great fun: Chirag Choudhary, Renee Moldovansky, Adam Pagon, Jenny Peterman, Rob Stein, Taran Eisler, Joe Boutros, Sam Boutros, Karim Botros, Tamiya Williams, Kathy Huff, Rhonda Fill, Rachel Rector, Antigone Castellucci, Erika Fedor, Tricia Bartram, Brittany Daddario, Sarah Strang, Wednesday Nelson, Kelly Liebler, Stephen Kaufman, Annie and Jason Klinefelter, KT and Kevin McCann, Patrick Howard, Kelly Stuber, Katelyn Hooper, Melissa Denham, Paul Turgeon, Mike Loy, Nick and Diana Prayson, David Harris, Rany Bous, Maged Guirgis, Mary Said Daryabigi, Mindy Dreher, Haley Webb, Evgenia Andrinopoulou, Leslee Segoviano, David Kaplan, Paul McMullen, Mary Ann Dugan, Jack and Barbara Reed, Adam Berebitsky, David Edelman, Maribel Gray and Chip Shaw.

Contents

Introduction

"Where in the world are you finding all these toilets, I've never seen one?!?!?"

"That's my favorite!!!"

"I've been looking every week driving around and still haven't seen any :("

"I want to be in the book!!!"

"I stayed up all night trying to think of a caption."

"OMG don't stop doing this!"

"When is the book coming out? I want to buy it."

When presented with comments and questions like these, how can one NOT write a book? At first it was unclear if there even could be such a thing. We had found four toilets in the wild within a month, but would there be more? The answer one month later was an emphatic YES! Apparently northeast Ohio and western Pennsylvania are riddled with toilets that are just waiting to be captured on film. The book became a reality.

Little did I realize how big the project would become. Ultimately, besides myself, there were 13 finders, 13 photographers, 17 prop suppliers, 10 title suppliers, 18 caption contributors, and 48 people in the caption and title contest group. Everyone was looking for toilets, thinking of ideas and props, or coming up with captions and titles. People were having fun and were actually excited about it. It was incredible.

The joy the project was bringing first became clear when I started getting toilet themed gifts e.g. a gold toilet float, having my office TP'd, toilet birthday cards, and toilets on my birthday cake. Furthermore, almost every new picture resulted in someone saying it was their favorite. That alone justified being on toilet call every day for almost a year, the long hours, and the scrambling to come up with a theme, props and photographer. Out of respect for the seriousness of the task, I tried to really pay attention to the details and had fun with the Easter eggs (e.g. movie and song references), so my recommendation to you, my reader, is to look at each picture closely and see what you can find.

A lot of people also really wanted to be in the book and not just see the pictures, so I promised anyone that found a toilet that was used, took a picture, or supplied a prop would be included. There were certain rules though:

1. **The toilet needed to be on the curb, out for pickup.** I wasn't going to go up next to someone's house for a picture.

2. **No setups or staged toilets!!** In other words, no putting toilets out on the curb to "find". My good friend Rob Stein was kind enough to offer to put two toilets in a bed of manure for me to find – no thank you!

3. **No Photoshop.** The only exceptions to this were to blur addresses and to brighten the photos for publication. This rule resulted a few times in having to go back to fix a prop or tuck a pocket back in.

4. **The toilet would be left as it lay.** There was one exception to this and that was *Porcelain Passion*. I needed to turn those two to face each other.

The fourth rule was the most frustrating while waiting for the cover picture. I had a goal of having 25 pictures but ended up with more while waiting for a whole, upright one to do the cover justice.

Originally my plan for the book was to try and share the experience of discovery and randomness by giving a history of each picture as the caption, but then Rachel and Mary pointed out my foolishness. Each picture would have a caption equivalent to: "Someone found a toilet, we got some props, we took a picture." That exciting narrative can now be found in the Appendix.

I decided instead that captions were the way to go. As hard as I tried, the captions I wrote just didn't feel right so I decided to reach out and see if there was any interest in another opportunity to get into the book. BAM! Over 40 people signed up for a caption and title contest. The members' enthusiasm, senses of humor and creativity crushed it and helped make this the book it is today.

Finally, the question everyone is asking now is, "what's next?" My answer is that it's up to you, the reader. My toilet journey is done, but if others want to carry on and send pictures (see instructions for submissions at www.bookofthrones.com) then maybe we'll have enough for "Number 2: Heirs to the Thrones".

Please enjoy the book.

Marc Estafanous

Porta Potty

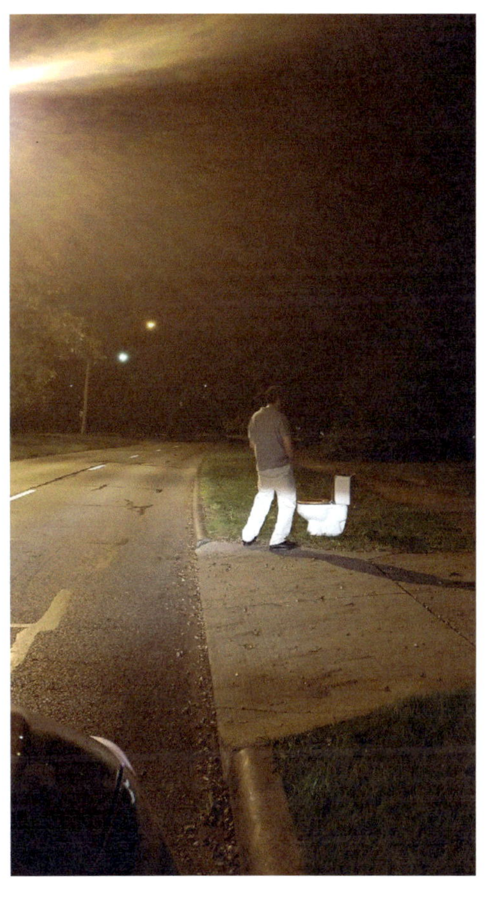

I didn't
make it
home.

Finder: Marc Estafanous
Photographer: Jessica French
Location: Cleveland Hts., OH
Date: August 18, 2018

Number 2

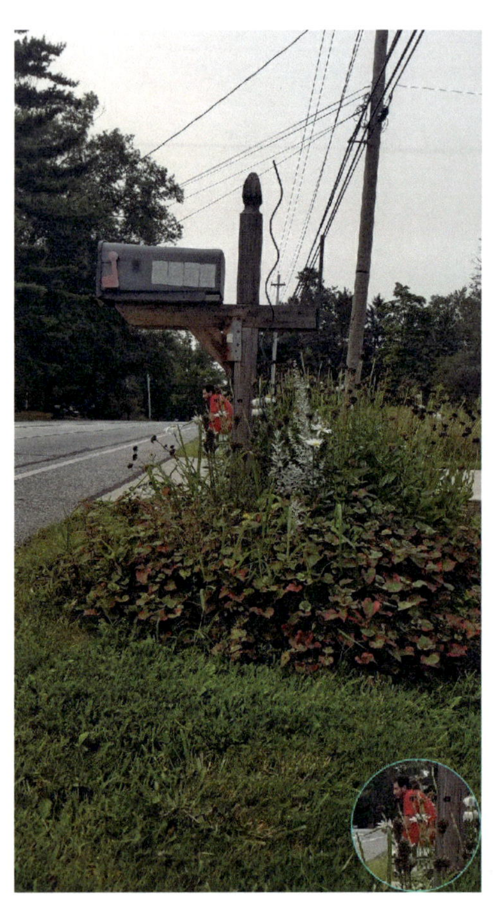

Privacy
please.

Finder:	Ken Bowman
Photographer:	Jessica French
Caption:	John Estafanous
Location:	Orange, OH
Date:	August 19, 2018

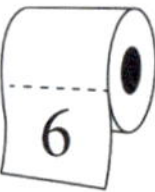

Upper Deckers

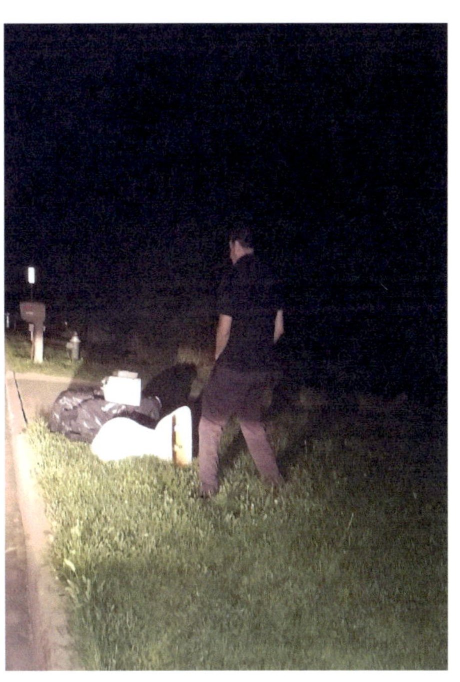

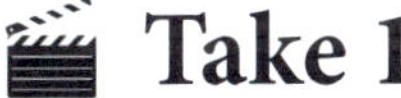 Take 1

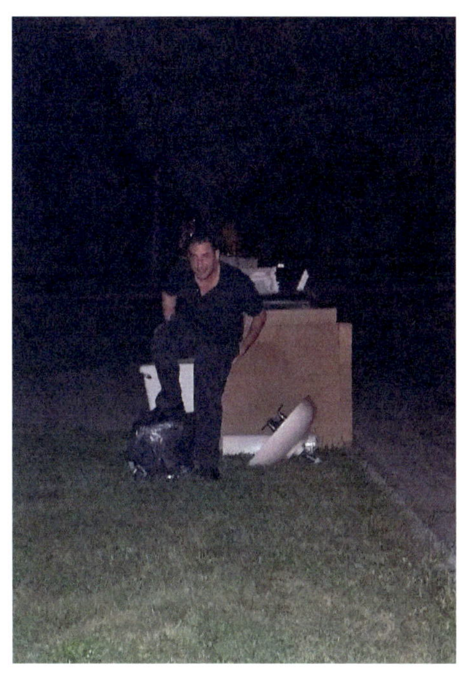 Take 2

Next level pooping.

Finders:	Jessica French and Marc Estafanous
Photographer:	Jessica French
Caption:	Stacey Nichols
Location:	Orange, OH
Date:	September 16, 2018

Wipe Right

6'0" SBP Captain looking for a fresh SWTP who doesn't mind getting down and dirty. Must like adventure, swimming, cave diving and exploring new places. Wrinkles ok, but must have soft skin. Come join me on an Interactive Safari!

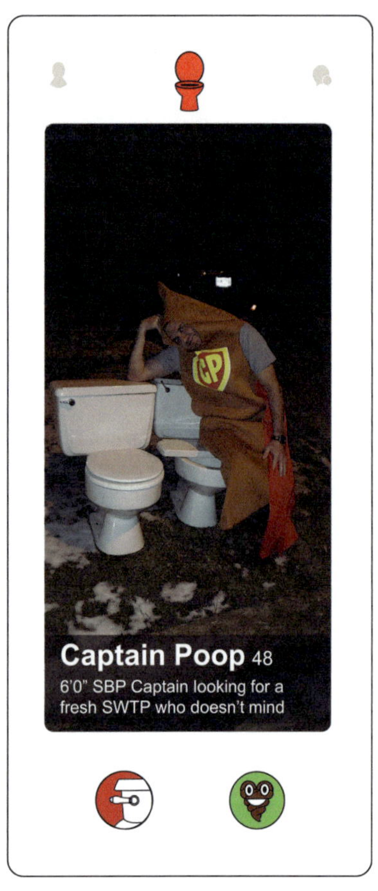

Finder:	Jackie LoPresti
Photographer:	Jackie LoPresti
Title:	Richard Marshall
Location:	Mayfield Hts., OH
Date:	December 12, 2018

Hot Tamales

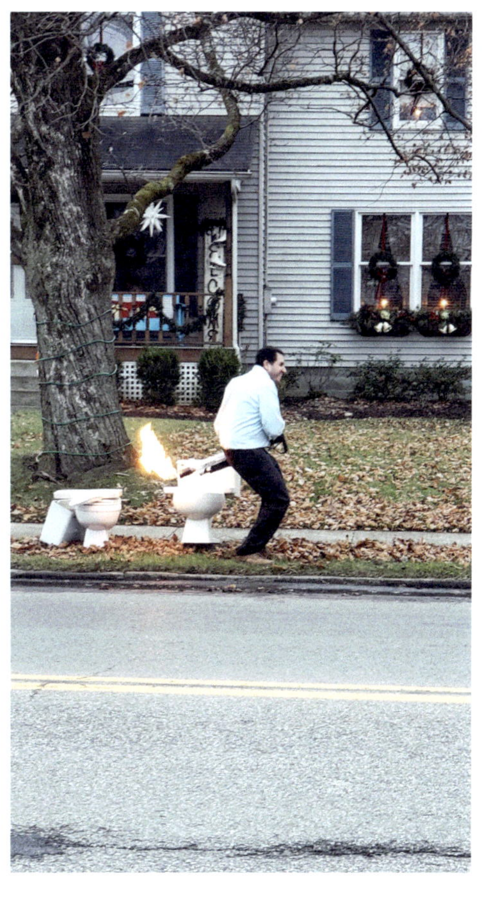

CAUTION:
Natural Gas
Explosion!

Finder: Tierra Sump
Photographer: Veronica Carkido
Prop Supplier: Elon Musk
Caption: Jen Trick
Location: Sharpsville, PA
Date: December 17, 2018

FAQ

Q: How in the world did you find all these toilets?!? I've never seen one!
A: That's almost always the very first question everybody asks me.
Evidently, they're not as rare as one would think in the northeast Ohio,
western Pennsylvania area. It also helped a lot that there were about 30
people on the lookout for toilets. People are still looking for them.

**Q: Did anyone ever confront you or call the police? Did you ask
permission?**
A: Yes, there was one time a lady yelled out to me from her door about
how the toilet was out for a special pick up the next day (*Bus Stop*), but the
police were never called. The pictures were always at the curb so nothing
illegal was being done since I never left extra garbage (except *No Hippos
Here*). I only asked for permission once (*I'm a Rockstar*). Finally, some
people honked but no one stopped.

Q: Are all of these different toilets?
A: Yes. They are all also pictured as they lay with the exception of *Porcelain
Passion* which required me to turn the two to face each other.

Q: What was your favorite part of the project?
A: Honestly, it was all fun. The best parts of the whole project however
were how many people were involved, how almost every picture resulted in
a new, "that's my favorite," and the sheer ridiculousness of the whole thing.

Q: Did you carry around your own toilets? Props?
A: No. These were all found in the wild. I did carry around some props like
the newspaper, the fish tank, and a few others. Most of the time I had to
scramble the night the subject was found before it disappeared.

Q: How much were the pictures edited?
A: Pictures were brightened and addresses and license plates were blurred.

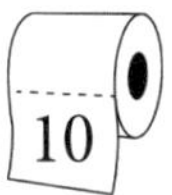

Morning Routine

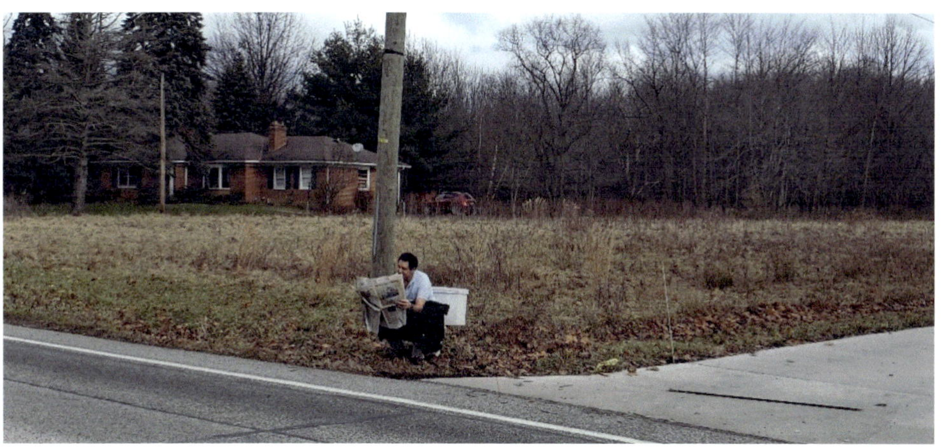

Serenity.

Finder:	Marc Estafanous
Photographer:	Ken Bowman
Caption:	Melissa Howard
Location:	Orange, OH
Date:	January 6, 2019

Trophy Kill

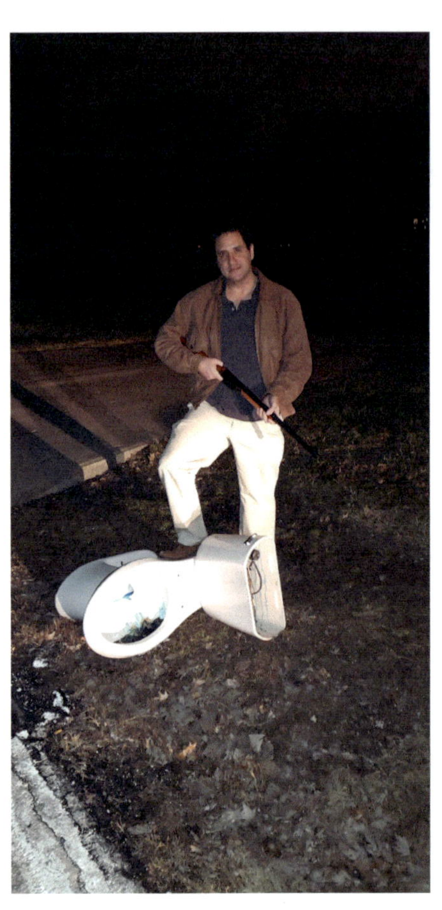

This will look great over my mantel.

Finder: Marc Estafanous
Photographer: Jackie LoPresti
Caption: Ken Bowman
Location: Mentor, OH
Date: March 2, 2019

Porcelain Passion

 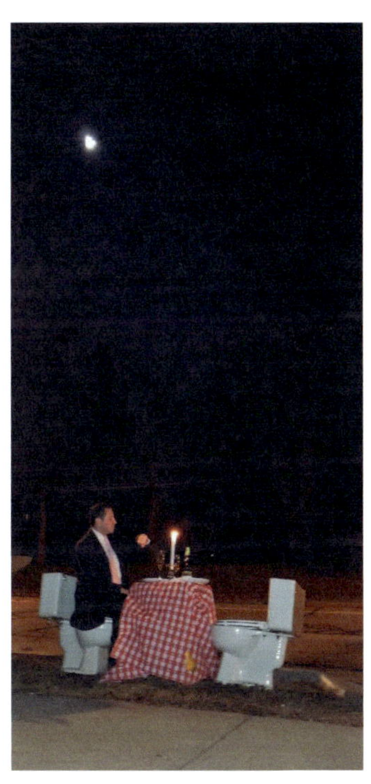

Ghosted again. Oh well.

Finder:	Bill Buehl-Reichard
Photographer:	Jackie LoPresti
Prop Supplier:	Fawzy Estafanous
Title:	Michael Dugan
Location:	Cleveland Hts., OH
Date:	March 19, 2019

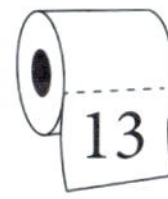

Potty Putter

Tee time.
Just tap
it in.

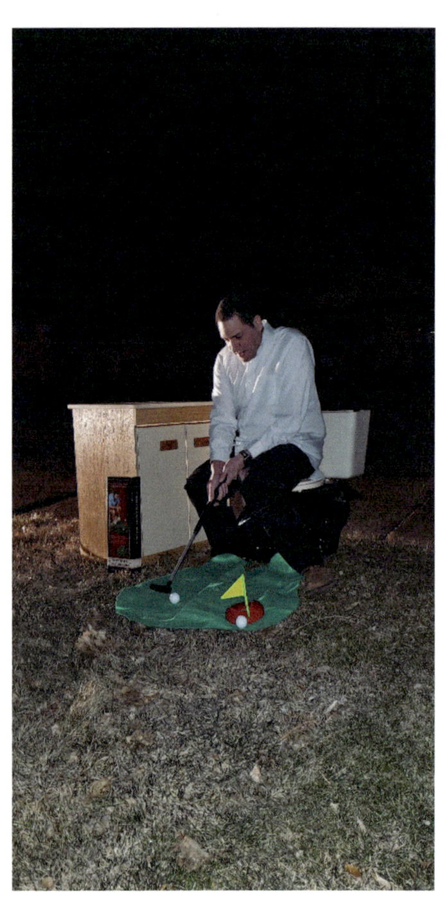

Finder: Marc Estafanous
Photographer: Jackie LoPresti
Prop Supplier: Shirley Zimmerman
Caption: Jackie LoPresti
Location: Mayfield Hts., OH
Date: March 19, 2019

Snaking the Pipes

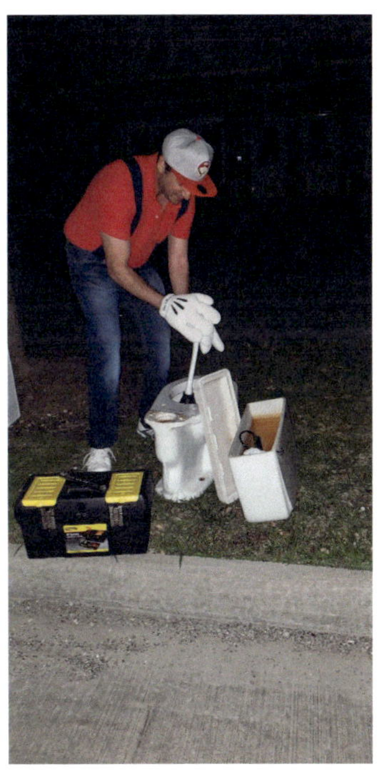

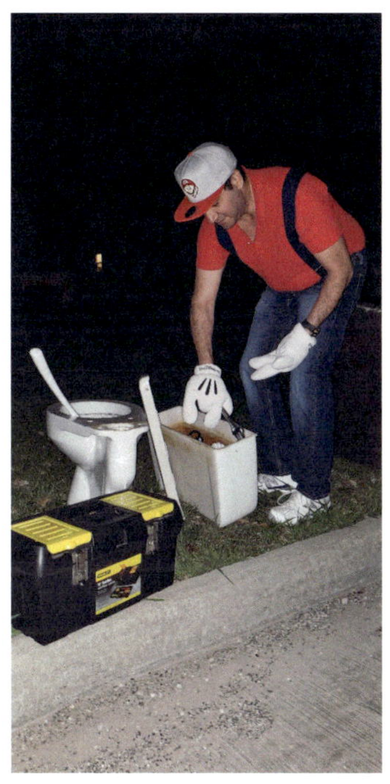

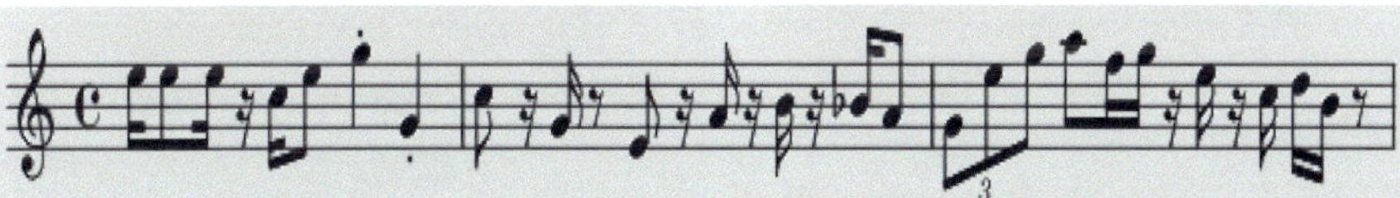

Today, full of energy,
Mario is still running, running
Go save Princess Peach! Go!
Today, full of energy, Mario runs

Today, full of energy, jumping!
Today, full of energy, searching for
   coins
Today, keep going, Mario! [1,2]

Finder: Jackie LoPresti
Photographer: Jackie LoPresti
Prop Supplier: Jackie LoPresti
Title: Ashley Zieminick
Location: Mayfield Hts., OH
Date: April 16, 2019

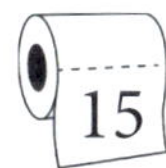

The Fishing Hole

Watch out
for
Poseiden's
kiss!

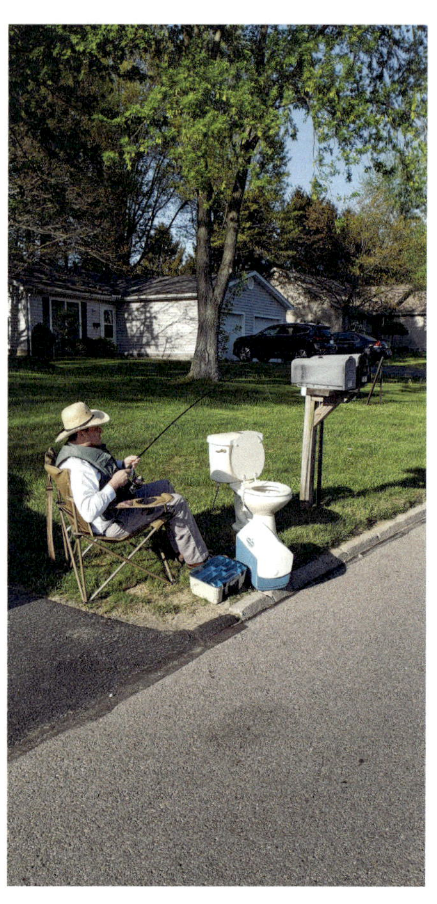

Finder: Shirley Zimmerman
Photographer: Josh Zimmerman
Prop Supplier: Josh Zimmerman
Caption: Marc Estafanous and Donnah Whitaker
Title John Estafanous
Location: Cortland, OH
Date: May 8, 2019

Picnic á la Commode

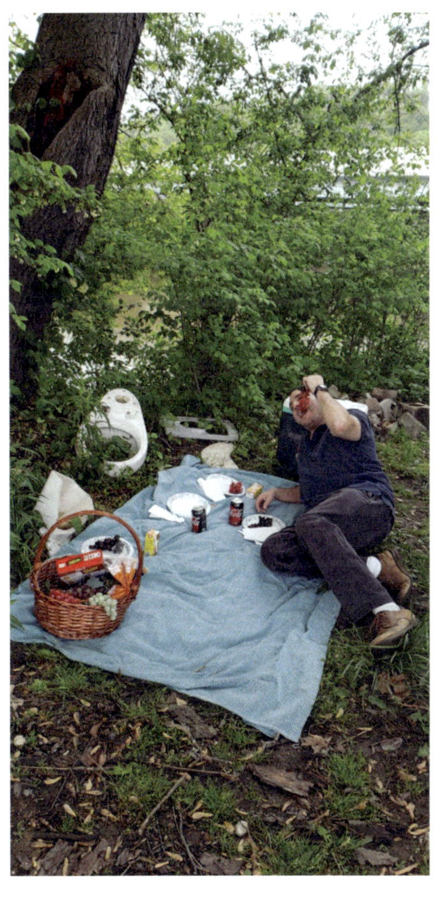

Might be
a couple
sandwiches
short of a
picnic!

Finder: Amanda Poole
Photographer: Amanda Poole
Prop Suppliers: Amanda Poole and Dara Briggs
Caption: Jill Hardy
Title: Jen Trick
Location: Uhrichsville, OH
Date: May 10, 2019

Trailcam

Nature's
calling.

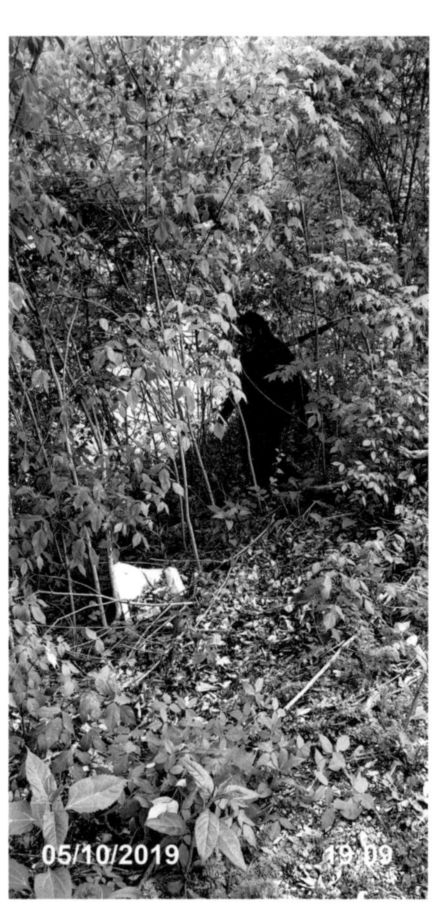

Finder: Amanda Poole
Photographer: Amanda Poole
Prop Supplier: Amanda Poole
Caption: Amanda Nagy
Location: Uhrichsville, OH
Date: May 10, 2019

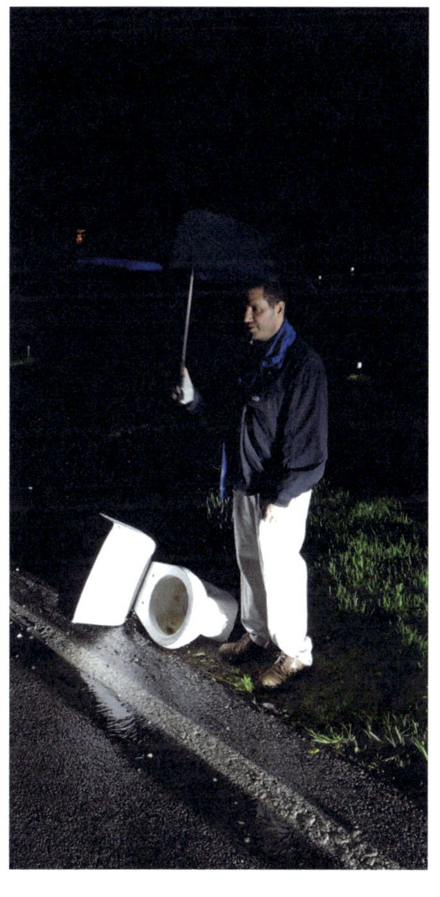

I'll stand
by you.

Finder: Jackie LoPresti
Photographer: Jackie LoPresti
Caption: Ashley Zieminick
Title: Jackie LoPresti
Location: Moreland Hills, OH
Date: May 12, 2019

Poop Selfie

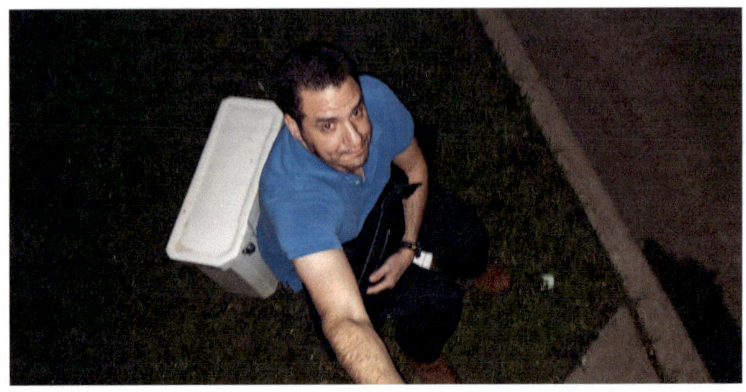

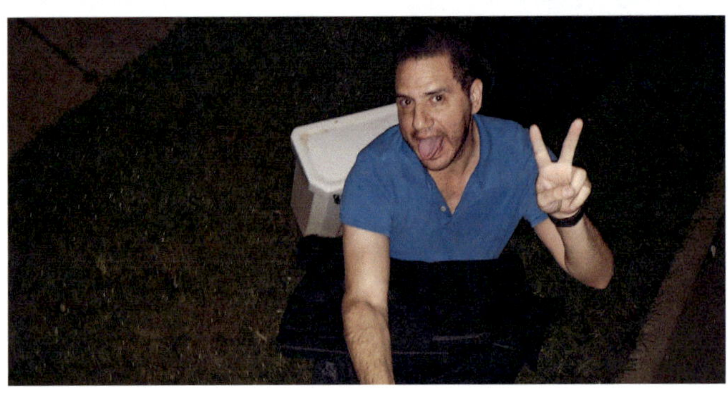

Give me a tbh.

Finder: Kevin Adelstein
Photographer: Marc Estafanous
Caption: Kim Smith
Title: Jessica French
Location: Solon, OH
Date: May 14, 2019

Playing with My Balls

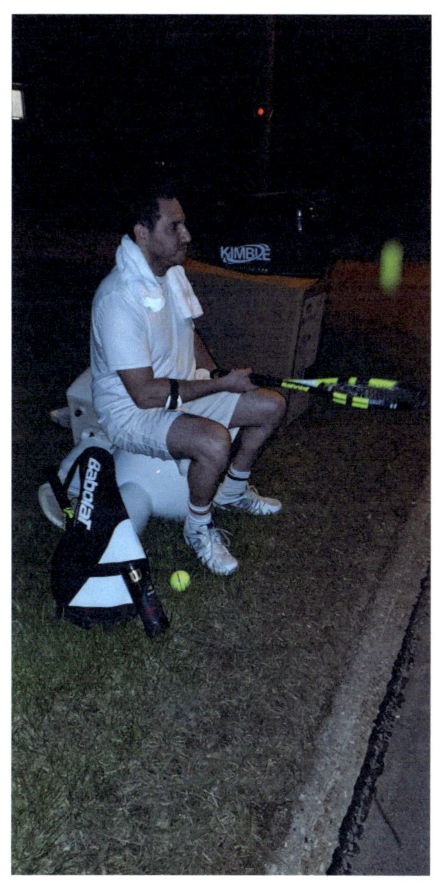

Spectacular
drop shots
are preceded
by spectacular
preparations.

Finder: Jackie LoPresti
Photographer: Brian Kraig
Caption: Don Brinberg and Ken Bowman
Title: Jackie LoPresti
Location: Flushing Meadows, New York
                 (Phil Mansour)
Date: May 16, 2019

Hula Poop

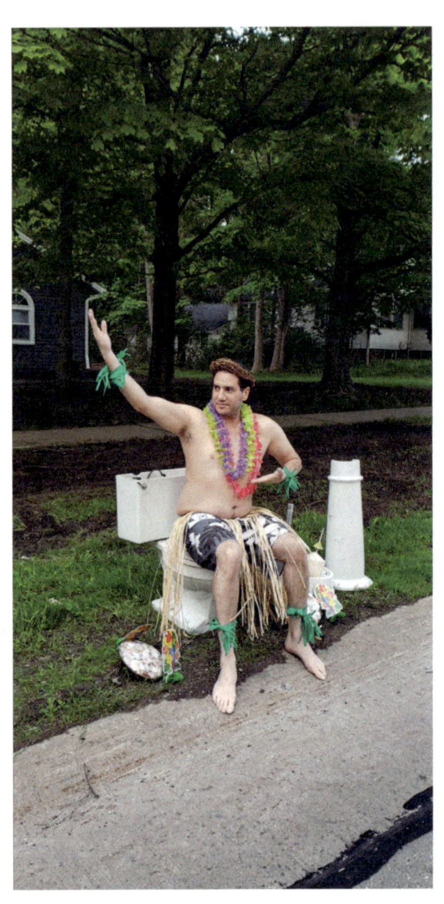

Getting lei'd before the eruption.

Finder:	Jackie LoPresti
Photographer:	Jackie LoPresti
Prop Supplier:	Veronica Carkido
Caption:	Taryn Jeffers
Title:	Richard Marshall
Location:	Mayfield Hts., OH
Date:	May 27, 2019

No Hippos Here

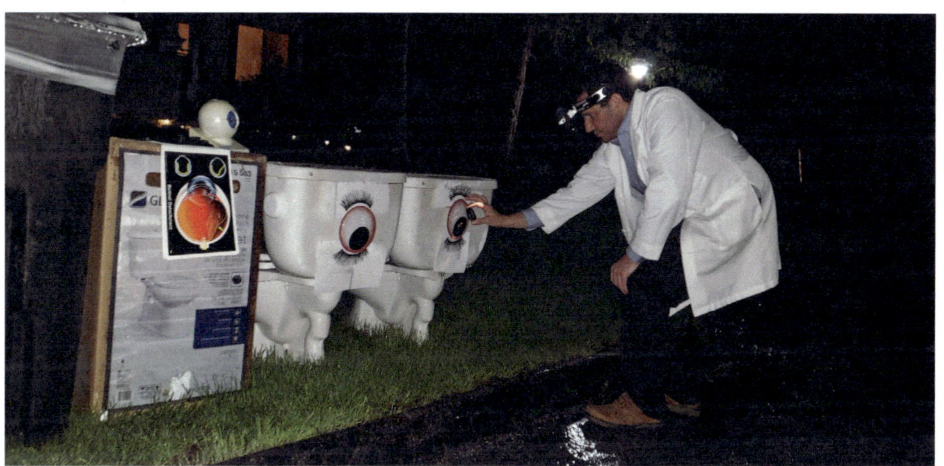

Trust me, I'm a doctor.

Finder:	Jackie LoPresti
Photographer:	Jackie LoPresti
Caption:	Dr. Pepper
Location:	Willoughby, OH
Date:	May 28, 2019

Free

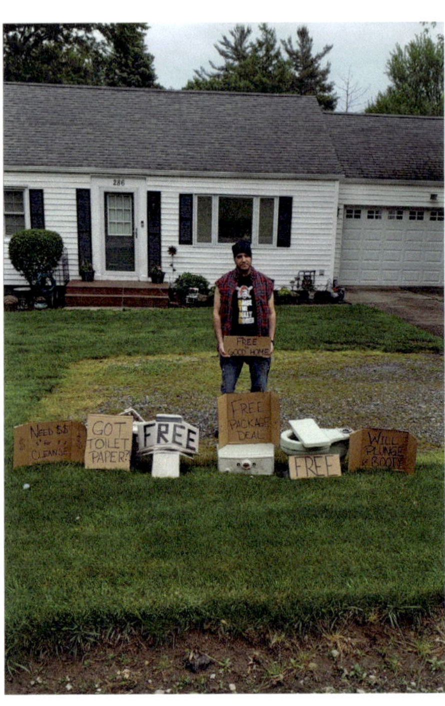

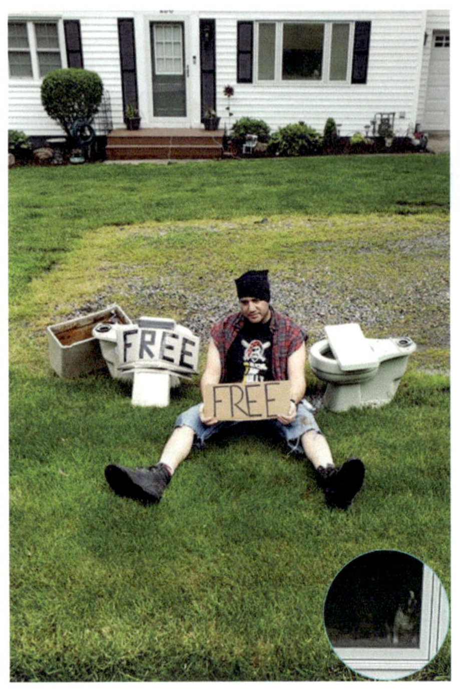

When your parents cut you off.

Finder:	Shirley Zimmerman
Photographer:	Ashley Zieminick
Prop Suppliers:	Ashley Zieminick and Tierra Sump
Caption:	Ashley Zieminick
Location:	Hermitage, PA
Date:	May 29, 2019

Flushing Hours

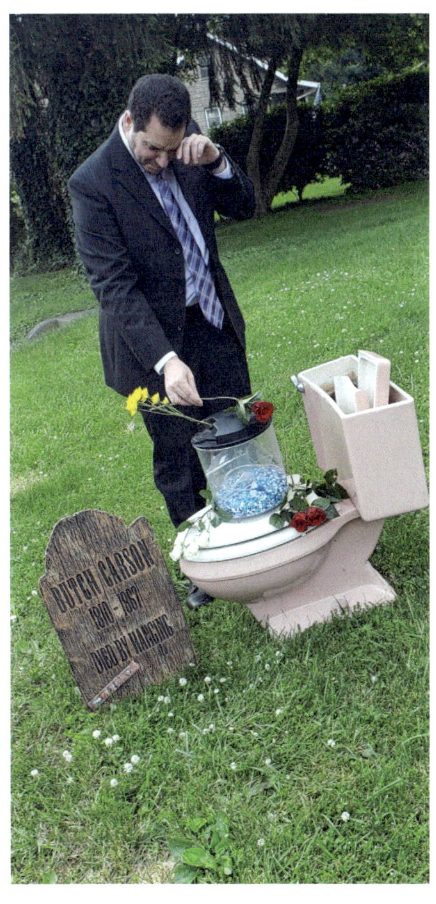

All drains lead
to the ocean.

Finder: Heather Vance
Photographer: Heather Vance
Prop Suppliers: Veronica Carkido, Nicol Mackall, and Nicole Lortz
Caption: Amanda Poole
Title: Phil Mansour
Location: Canton, OH
Date: May 30, 2019

The Tea Party

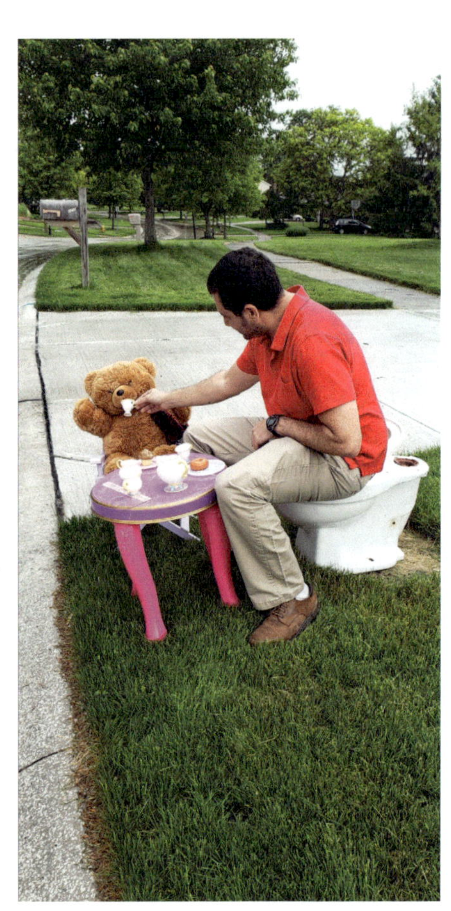

One lump
or two?

Finder: Sammi Steindler
Photographer: Sammi Steindler
Prop Suppliers: Rachel and Mary Estafanous
Caption: Ashley Zieminick
Location: Solon, OH
Date: June 1, 2019

You Spin Me Right Round

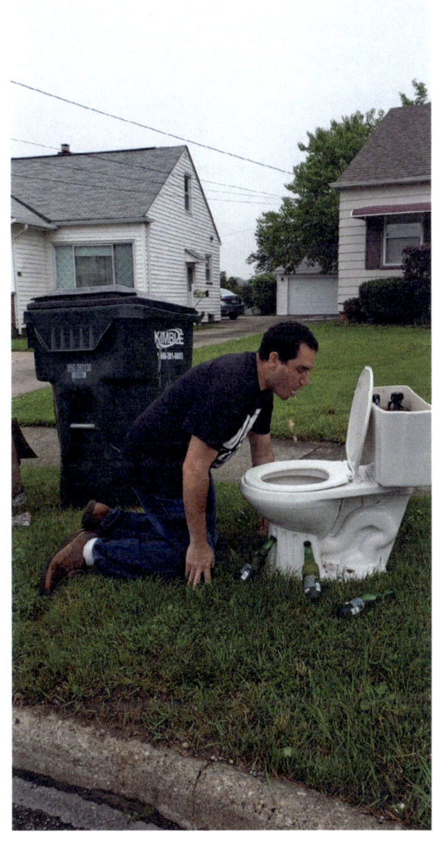

Praying
to the
Porcelain
Goddess.

Finder: Jahadge Floyd
Photographer: Mary Estafanous
Prop Supplier: Rachel Estafanous
Caption: Beth Nielsen
Location: Garfield Heights, OH
Date: June 16, 2019

Corbet's Couloir

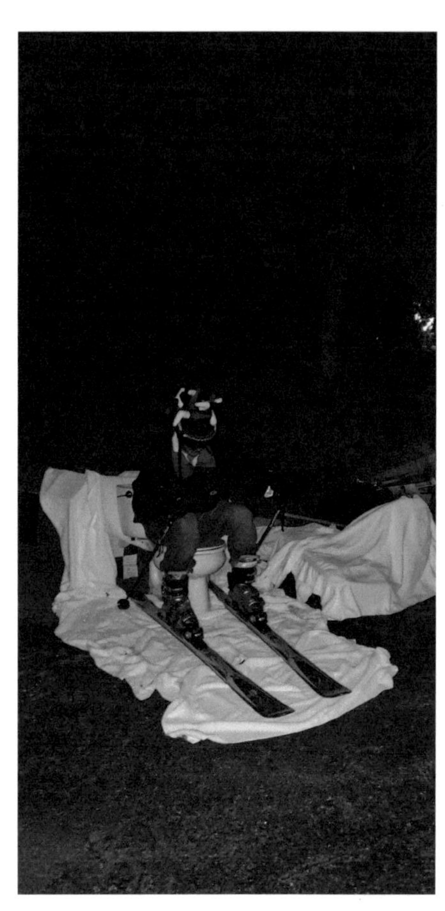

Prepping for the 20 foot drop.

Finder: Marc Estafanous
Photographer: John Abdelsayed
Location: Solon, OH
Date: June 17, 2019

I'm a Rockstar

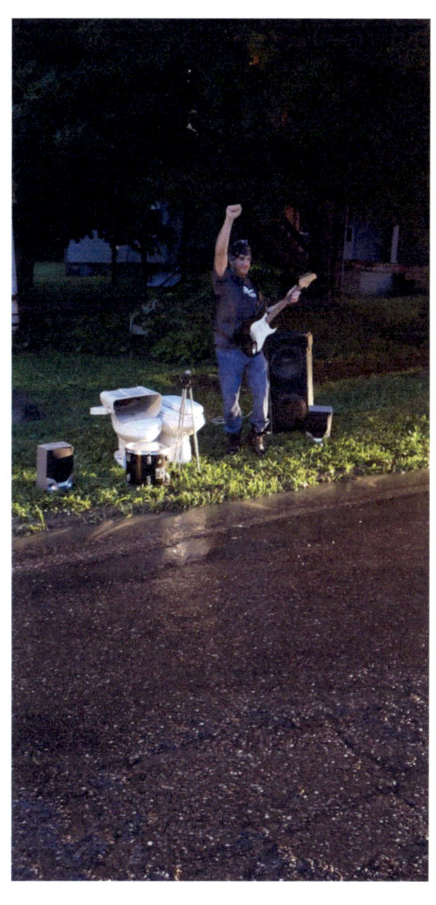

"I wanna rock and roll all night, and potty every day!"

Finder: Amanda Poole
Photographer: Amanda Poole
Prop Suppliers: Amanda Poole and Dara Briggs
Caption: Howard Krantz
Location: Uhrichsville, OH
Date: June 20, 2019

Float Like a Butterfly...

Sting like a bee.

Standing against me is completely absurd. I'm the greatest!

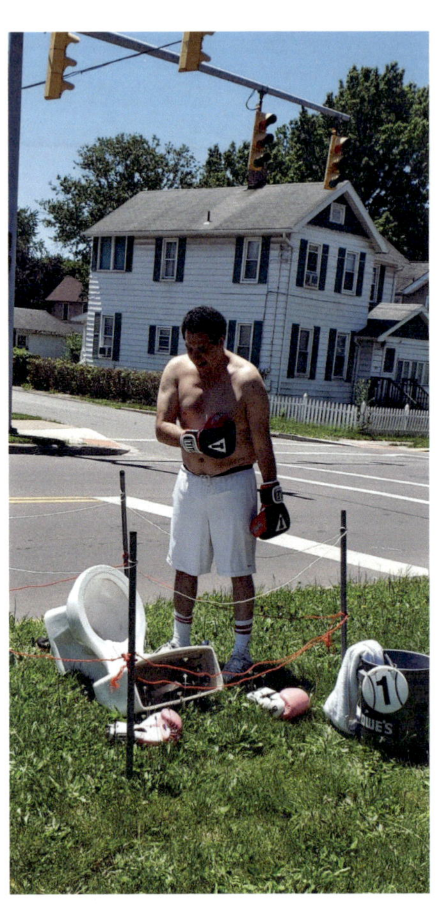

Finder:	Veronica Carkido
Photographer:	Veronica Carkido
Prop Suppliers:	Troy Budgen, Rachel & Mary Estafanous, Veronica Carkido
Caption/Title:	Muhammad Ali
Location:	Girard, OH
Date:	June 23, 2019

Party Pooper

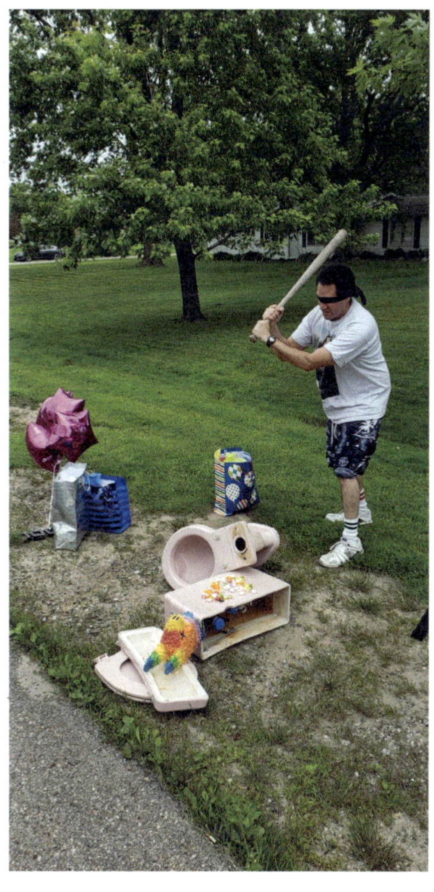

Sadly, the candy was crap.

Finder: Marc Estafanous
Photographer: Cory Nichols
Prop Suppliers: Stacey and Cory Nichols
Caption: Andrew Smith
Title: Mary Estafanous
Location: Streetsboro, OH
Date: June 24, 2019

The King of Thrones

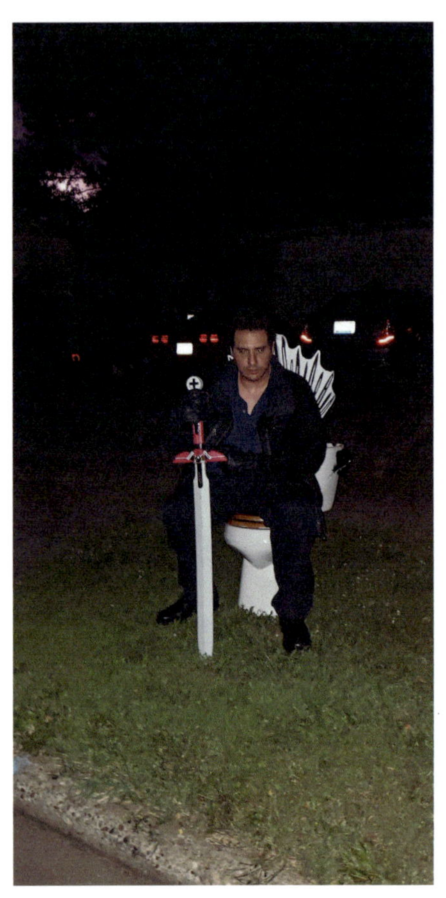

Who needs the Iron Throne?

Finder: Jill Hardy
Photographer: Mary Estafanous
Prop Supplier: Lucas Estafanous
Caption: Richard Marshall
Location: Massillon, OH
Date: June 29, 2019

More FAQs

Q: What's the furthest you've traveled for a picture?
A: 1.5 hours (*Picnic á la Commode* and *Trailcam*).

Q: How do you come up with the themes?
A: Each toilet speaks to me. Plus I have a lot of creative and fun friends
that had a ton of good suggestions. I did scramble though for most
of the props and ideas. The opportunities came in streaks so I wasn't
prepared for all of them.

Q: How many did you miss?
A: I was told about six or seven toilets after they were already gone.

Q: How did you take the pictures?
A: All the pictures were taken with cell phones (a Galaxy S7 and
a Galaxy S9+). Lots of pictures were taken for each theme and the
favorite was chosen for the book by whoever was present. Extra
pics and 'making of' videos can be found on the website: www.
bookofthrones.com.

Q: Which is your favorite?
A: I don't have just one. I love *Trophy Kill* because of the Red Ryder BB
gun. *Porcelain Passion* was great because of the full moon, the look on
my dad's face when I showed him the pictures, and the pure audacity
of setting up the table and having a drink on the side of the street.
Trailcam I love because of the 'wait for it' aspect of the pic. Finally, how
can I not love *The King of Thrones* after having driven an hour with
Mary for the coup d'etat with the LIGHTNING in the background?!?

Q: What's next?
A: Well, I got tired of being on daily toilet call, so my days of toilet
chasing are done. If there is enough interest I am happy to work with
others to continue the fun.

Appendix

Porta Potty
One night, on the way home after dinner, Jess, and I saw something on the side of the road and we laughed. I turned to her and said, we have to get a picture of that. "Absolutely," she said. We circled around the block and we had found our first porta potty. We texted the group and Dmitry replied, "All is great except you didn't want to go number 2."

Number 2
The very next day Ken texted a picture of a toilet to the group with the comment: "Good thing I went before I left for Lowe's or I would have had to pull a 'Marc' in broad daylight." Jess and I were on it! To answer the question that Dmitry asked after seeing the picture, the answer is leaves.

Upper Deckers
A month later and lo and behold we found two toilets on the same street! Neither was amenable to sitting on them directly and Jess had the great idea of the upper deckers.

Chris: "You guys… it's like a new hobby."
Ken: "I would keep the pictures and make a 'bathroom book' out of it that people keep in their bathrooms. Pulitzer idea right there."

And the adventure began!

Wipe Right
Nothing for almost three months. The idea of a book had started to fade. Then all of sudden I got a late text from Jackie: "I found a double!" I knew just what to do.

I have a policy of dressing up as whatever my children ask me to dress up as for Halloween. The costumes have ranged from Justin Bieber, to Papa Smurf, to a whoopee cushion. Unfortunately for two Halloweens I donned the above Captain Poop costume. The last time my daughter didn't even go trick or treating, she and her friend just walked around reviewing biology, using me as a mascot and a reference when they had a question. It was time to don the costume again.

I thought it must be lonely being a Single Brown Poop, and I was right, he's looking for the right Single White Toilet Paper.

Mini FAQ
Q: What is an Interactive Safari?
A: It's a term I coined. It's a date on which you feel like you're in a different country with a different species but you're part of the show.

Hot Tamales
It's a Sunday night a few days later and Tierra texts: "double toilet in Sharpsville." There's a risk that it might be gone, but there's no time before work on Monday. Veronica stepped up to take the picture. It's rush hour, cars are driving by nonstop, Veronica is across the street, and I have my frigging FLAME THROWER out. Not a single honk, no cops. It's like nothing is happening. It's amazing what the internet has gotten us all accustomed to. It was hilarious and awesome.

Morning Routine
This one I thought I was ready for. I knew I had to take one with the morning paper and it was less than a week after I got a paper that this toilet popped up, not even two houses from *Number 2*. The problem turned out to be that I didn't have anyone with me to take the picture when I found it and I was scheduled to see a movie.

I actually had a nightmare about just this situation. I was driving down the road and saw a toilet on the left, turned to my right and the car was empty. Then I saw another toilet, and another, and then I woke up. Whew!! It really was just a dream.

I reached out and fortunately, Ken came to the rescue. We grabbed the picture and I made it on time to the movie.

Trophy Kill
After another two month dry spell, I was on call on the way to my office

and there it was. I pulled over to get the address and saw how gross it was on the inside. When I saw it at first on its side I had thought I'd lie against it or something but no way, too nasty! No worries though, I knew just what I needed to do. There were no photographers available again though so I headed home, grabbed a phone holder and was all set to selfie it.

I tried a couple of pics and it was failing. Then Jackie came and bailed me out. I was lucky I didn't shoot my eye out.

Porcelain Passion

Another double!! Bill texted me in the middle of the day, and all I could do was hope that they wouldn't be gone in the evening. Jackie had had a great idea for a night out on the town so I called her up and luckily she was free. I stopped by a party supply store and got a table cloth and a candle holder. I then went to my dad's and grabbed the table. This one was perfect with the full moon for the win.

I took the table back to my dad, showed him the pictures and all he could do was shake his head. Some people will never understand art.

Potty Putter

I had just dropped Jackie off and was heading back down her street after getting the *Porcelain Passion* pics, when there it was, a toilet with a vanity! In the literally five minutes it took to drive half a block back and forth and let her out of the car, magic happened. I immediately called, "Jackie! Don't go to bed, I need you again!"

I was lucky, Shirley had given me a Potty Putter for a pic and so I had it handy in the car. Whew! That was almost a swing and a miss.

Snaking the Pipes

What is it with Mayfield Heights? So many toilets!! This one was broken though and it was late. We needed a plumber. Who else can fix a destroyed toilet besides the best plumber in the world? We needed Mario! Who knew his theme song had words?!?

No suspenders or hat so a quick trip to Walmart in the middle of the night. Score! They had a Mario hat in addition to the suspenders. That combined with the Mickey Mouse gloves that Jackie had and Mario was in the house.

The Fishing Hole

Ugh, far from home, on the way back from work and Shirley tells me about another one. What to do? Josh offered to be the photographer. We had planned on a fishing pic and Josh had all the right props. In addition to the hat, jacket and rod, I'll take that chair, the cooler, and that tackle box. Oh, and let me tie a rock to the line to bend the pole. Perfect.

Mini FAQ

Q: What is Poseidon's Kiss?
A: It's the splashback.

This was the first time someone watched. The owner was on her cell and looking through the screen while we cleaned up. No confrontation this time but a friend of Shirley's texted her later and told her she saw us taking the picture.

Picnic á la Commode and Trailcam

Amanda had found a toilet in the woods while canoeing a couple of weeks before. I finally had the perfect idea for it and I couldn't believe she had the perfect prop for it. While she was looking for a closer place to put the canoe into the water she found the broken gem for a picnic. It was worth the hour and a half drive for the twofer.

Seriously though, how did Amanda have this prop just lying around?

Bus Stop

Finally a confrontation! It was raining, and there I was on the side of the road with a tripod. The owner of the house walks out of her door, and two guys are looking through windows.

Owner: "They're picking that up tomorrow!"
Me: "OK"
Owner: "But they're picking that up tomorrow!"
Me: "I'm just taking a picture."
Owner: "Why?"
Me: "For my toilet book."
Crickets…

The self shot video/pics didn't really work. Jackie stepped up once again and we went back and got the pic.

Poop Selfie
Kevin alerted me to a subject in the early evening. I already had plans to see a late movie. There were too many pictures in a row so it was selfie time. I had hoped to get a side shot of the process and Rachel came out but the lighting just wasn't right. I went back at 2 am after the movies and luckily my newly bought selfie stick was still charged. I never cared for poop selfies, but this one I couldn't resist.

Playing with My Balls
What a week! Jackie was a toilet finding beast. She found it in Mayfield Heights, and obviously not in Flushing Meadows, where the US Open is played. This was the sixth toilet in eight days and her fourth. The book was on a roll and looked like it might just become a reality. I had just finished playing tennis and had the foresight to borrow some towels and bring some balls before I went to talk to Brian. I asked if he was bored and he was like, "let's go".

The lady across the street came out with her dog, watched us for a minute and said, "You guys are weird." The dog started barking and the lady of the house started watching us. There's nothing like a little adrenaline to improve your game.

Hula Poop
Pat Catan's was going out of business and I was told I might find a good outfit there for my cover picture. Unfortunately almost everything was sold out until I found this gem of a getup. Veronica helped me find everything and got the

missing wrist and ankle pieces. I got the coconut at an Asian festival a few days before and had been praying it wouldn't rot.

Jackie came through again on the same street as *Playing with My Balls.* Seriously, what is it with Mayfield Heights? There was a teenager mowing the grass at the house next door. He didn't even notice us.

No Hippos Here
Seriously, it's like Jackie has a toilet finding super power. Little did I know it was the start of another streak. Another double but this time they were facing the wrong way. I knew exactly what needed to be done. They were obviously having trouble seeing. I looked for tears and detachments but didn't find any.

The best part of this picture, besides having to wait between downpours to take it, was that it was in the front of an apartment/townhome development; so we left the eyes. I would've paid a lot of money to see the reactions.

Mini FAQ
Q: Why the title No Hippos Here?
A: If you're a parent, you may have read the picture and sound book, "Animal Adventure" (Catherine McCafferty, 1999). On every page we were looking for a hippo. Each time we didn't find one we pressed a button which exclaimed, "no hippos here!" I read it too many times so at the end of surgeries when I was looking for any tears, much to the dismay of my nurse Kathy, I got into the habit of saying, "no hippos here."

Free
Ashley really wanted to be a part of the book. She texted me while I was in surgery because Shirley had found another pair. These toilets were special for a few reasons. Firstly, the week before Don was complaining that I had all white toilets and that there weren't any pastel colored ones. He pointed to a pale green color on the wall as an example and said there should be pink ones too. The one on the right was exactly the green color he pointed to!

Secondly, who would ever take free toilets?!? The theme was obvious. Ashley grabbed clothes from Goodwill, she and Tierra tore them up, rubbed them in mud and made signs. We even had a doggy audience. Priceless.

Flushing Hours
Heather found this one and I had been carrying around a fish bowl just in case. What I didn't do was carry around a suit. Nicol borrowed her fiancé's and we were in business. Bonus points too for being the second pastel in a row thus satisfying Don's demands for green and pink toilets.

The Tea Party
Sammi: I found a toilet.
Me: Great where?
Sammi: Solon, but it's tiny.
Me: Wth does that mean?
Sammi: It just seems tiny to me.
Me: OK, I got this, I had daughters. See you soon.

You Spin Me Right Round
Beth is a smart, sophisticated, beautiful woman who was full of ideas. Given her professionalism, I obviously had to go with praying to the Porcelain Goddess.

Unfortunately, I didn't have anyone to hold my hair up for me as I was losing my lunch, but Mary, Rachel and Jahadge were more than happy to record my pain. Kids these days.

Mini FAQ
Q: Is that real puke?
A: Maybe

Corbet's Couloir
Luckily the final streak had started. I found this one on the way home. Lots of boxes around it and it was hot. So hot that I had to pull out my ski gear to try and lose a few pounds of water weight. Corbet's Couloir is a famous jump in Jackson

Hole, Wyoming that I've always wanted to do. The problem is that I'd poop my pants on the way down. Luckily John was up late.

I'm a Rock Star
I was done. All I needed was my cover picture and then no more toilet call. Then Amanda called again. Another double. They sang to me so it was natural to work with them in a band. Amanda and Dara came through once again with the props, and Goodwill came through again with the clothes. These were literally ten feet away from the front door though and the door was open with a family of three inside. I finally ended up asking for permission for some pictures and they enjoyed watching the foolishness.

Float Like a Butterfly...
Veronica found another bonus one that wouldn't do for the cover picture and it was an extra hour of driving. That toilet pissed me off. It learned its lesson.

Party Pooper
I started to wonder, would the bonuses never end? Would I be on call forever? What better way to keep partying after a birthday party?

The King of Thrones
Finally!!! My toilet finding network pulled through again. I didn't even know Jill was looking! It turned out it was another 'free' toilet and it was upright and ready to go, but a storm was brewing and it was an hour away. Mary was ready to go. I had everything I needed: the clothes, an extra cape, scepter and crown if need be, a raven, my sword throne, and my sword. We were off and hoping we wouldn't get drenched.

On the way down there was a crazy lightning storm right in the direction we were heading. I told Mary, "God is blessing this book if we get the lightning in the picture." God blessed it, and she nailed it!

References

1. "Super Mario Bros. theme." Wikipedia: The Free Encyclopedia. Wikimedia Foundation, Inc. 22 July 2004. Web. 1 July 2019, https://en.wikipedia.org/wiki/Super_Mario_Bros._theme

2. "The Mario Bros. Theme Has Lyrics". Kotaku. December 1, 2015. https://kotaku.com/the-mario-bros-music-has-official-lyrics-1745593728

3. Cover Map created at: https://mapstyle.withgoogle.com/ with the stock Dark Theme

About the Author

Marc Estafanous, MD is a vitreo-retinal surgeon and this is his first book publication. In addition to being published in medicine, he has been published for his work on the mathematics of blackjack and programmed MGP's Blackjack CA. When he is not chasing toilets he is usually enjoying time with his children, on the tennis courts, skiing, programming his practice's EHR, or working on his Neurobaby®.

You can reach him via email at king@bookofthrones.com and on Facebook as BookOf Thrones.

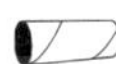

QED

Made in the USA
Monee, IL
07 July 2026

56553281R00033